The Abor

Snowman

written by
Tytus Huffman

illustrated by
Gary Rees

Macdonald

From the Himalayan Mountains of Nepal and Tibet to the forests of Western America come stories of mysterious creatures. Explorers travelling through these lands, and the people who live there too, say they have seen large hairy animals walking upright like men. People have followed strange tracks in the snow. They have heard strange cries at night. No large apes are known to live in America, but a man there took a twenty-second film of an ape-like creature. Another American toured his country with a hairy figure frozen in a block of ice.

What creatures did the explorers and local people see? What animals made the tracks in the snow? Are the film and the figure in ice proof that unknown beings exist? Is there any proof that a hairy creature like a large ape, that walks upright, lives in distant corners of the world?

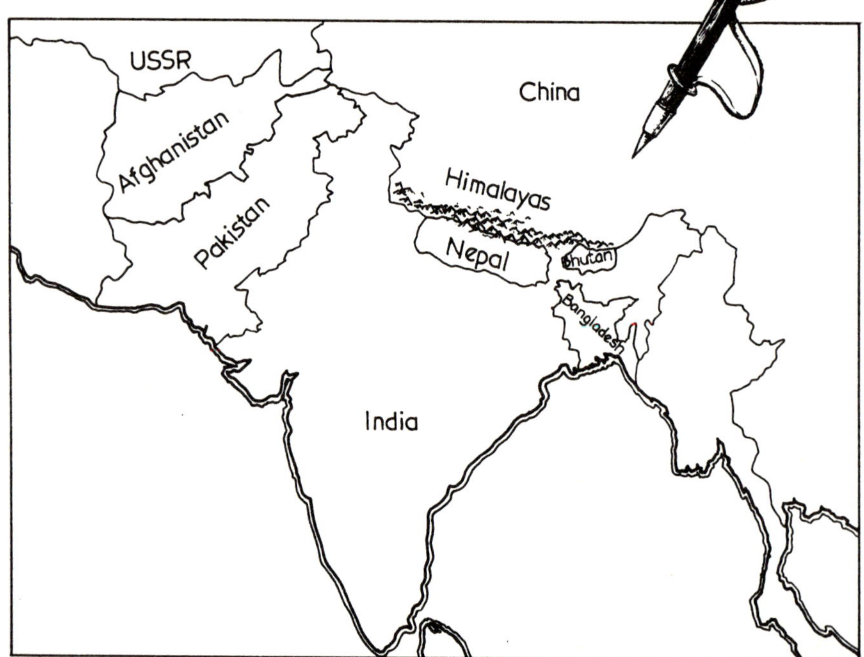

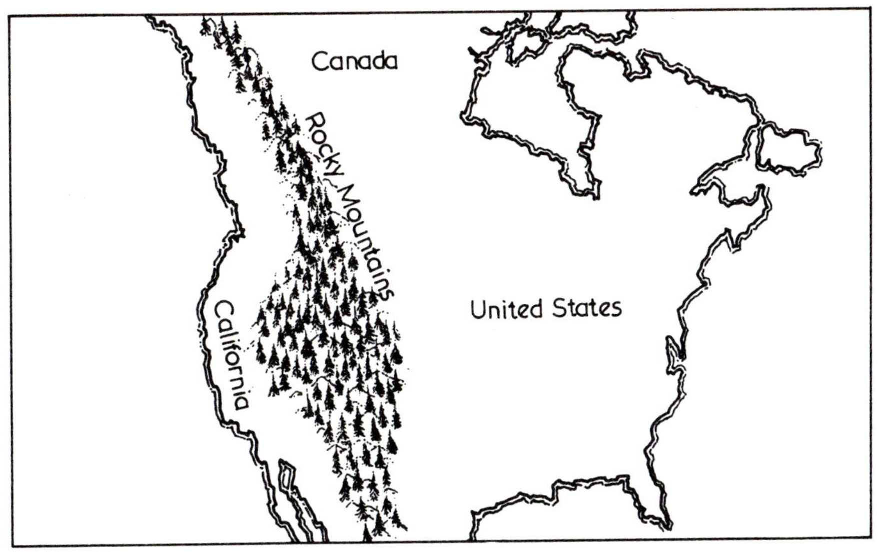

The Sherpas who live in Nepal, believe there is such an animal in the Himalayas. They call it *yeti* or *metch-kangmi*. That means 'abominable snowman'. American Indians say there is an ape-like creature in their own forests. They call it a *sasquatch*, or 'wild man of the woods'. Sometimes the same creature is called a *bigfoot*. Although the Himalayas are the opposite side of the world to America, the yeti and the sasquatch would seem to be very much alike.

The American Indians wear a costume for special dances, which may look rather like a sasquatch. It has an ape-like face. Its lips are puckered as though for whistling. The costume is covered with reddish hair. As the drums beat the Indians dance with their arms dangling down.

The Sherpas say that the yeti is covered with reddish hair too. It has an ape-like face and short neck. Its arms are long and muscular. It walks upright. Sherpas say that it whistles to other yetis.

Abominable snowmen are known to Europeans too. A member of the British Royal Geographical Society was in the Himalayas in 1925. At a height of 5,000 metres he saw a hairy man-like creature 200 metres away. The explorer watched it for several minutes. Then it walked away on two legs. In 1930 another Englishman was camping in the mountains. He heard shrill cries at night and his guides fled. At daylight the explorer saw strange footprints around his tent.

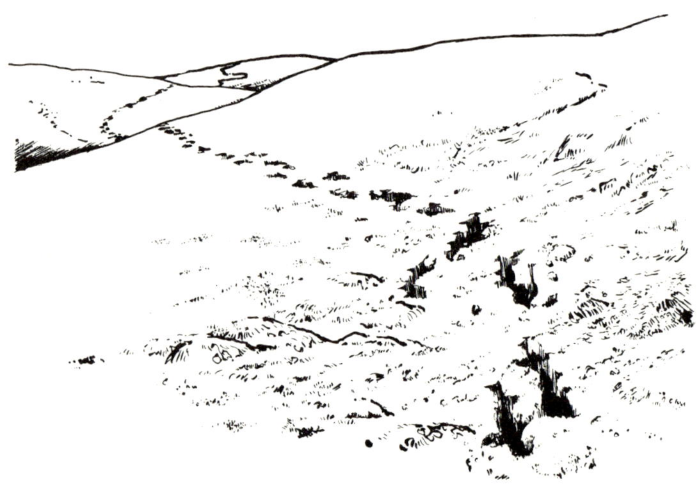

Sherpas have told explorers of their fights with snowmen. Monks in the mountain monasteries said how they frightened the beings away at night with gongs and trumpets. There were certainly many people, both Europeans and people living in the Himalayas, who said they had seen yetis. So far, however, no one had even photographed its tracks.

Then in 1951 Eric Shipton and Edmund Hillary went to the Himalayas. They were experienced mountain climbers and planned to study Mount Everest. Shipton was alone one day, at a height of 6,000 metres. There was a line of footprints in the snow. They looked as though they had been made by a big two-legged creature. Shipton photographed them in the bright sun. The marks were 33 centimetres long and 20 centimetres wide. Each print showed a giant big toe and four smaller ones. There were no claw marks like the ones bears would make.

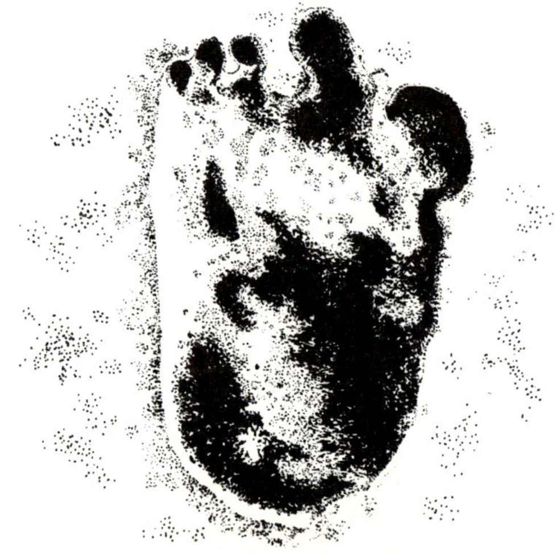

Shipton showed his photographs in Europe. Scientists could not identify the footprints. Some of them began to think that there might well be an unknown animal in the Himalayas that walked upright.

In America explorers had been seeing the same tracks. David Thomson had written in his diary about even bigger footprints. That was in 1811 near the Columbia River. Later, people on America's West Coast reported many prints just as big.

Canadians and Americans began to see signs of sasquatches and bigfoot also. In 1870 a hunter told Californian reporters that he had seen two hairy beings destroy his fire. The creatures had long arms and short legs. They were both big and whistled to each other.

After they had put out his campfire they walked away upright. All this time the hunter was hiding in the bushes. He was too afraid to shoot.

Lumberjacks chopping down trees had met bigfoot in the woods. Road builders had reported their lorries overturned at night. Fishermen had spoken of lines pulled out of their hands by hairy creatures rising out of the water nearby. There have been no end of strange sightings in America!

By 1967 bigfoot were so well known in California that Roger Patterson set out to make a film of them. When he returned from his expedition, he had an exciting story to tell. He said that he had been riding through the woods when he came to a small clearing. At first it looked very quiet, and then he noticed a movement over to his left. He was about to get down and investigate when, suddenly, a huge creature stepped out right in front of him. He reached for his camera, but his horse reared up in fright and threw him to the ground. Even though he was bruised and shaken, he managed to make a 20-second film of the animal before it disappeared back into the trees. Its face was turned to the camera. Its arms seemed longer than a human's. To Patterson the animal looked almost three metres tall.

At the same time another American was showing to the public a two-legged creature in ice. The man said it was found in the Bering Straits. The figure was man-sized and hairy. Its feet and hands were big. Its face was flat. Scientists examined it as closely as the owner would let them. Several thought that it might be an unknown type of man. They said it might even be a yeti.

By now it seemed there might possibly be abominable snowmen somewhere in the world. In 1935 a Dutch scientist had discovered a giant fossil jaw in southern China. The jaw was twice as big as a gorilla's. The teeth were half human, half ape. The scientist called the creature *Gigantopithecus*. He said it must have been at least three metres tall and have weighed 252 kilograms. Instead of eating fruit and leaves like gorillas, it ate grain. It lived long ago in open country near the Himalayas and may have walked upright. The description of the giant fitted the yeti. Was Gigantopithecus still alive?

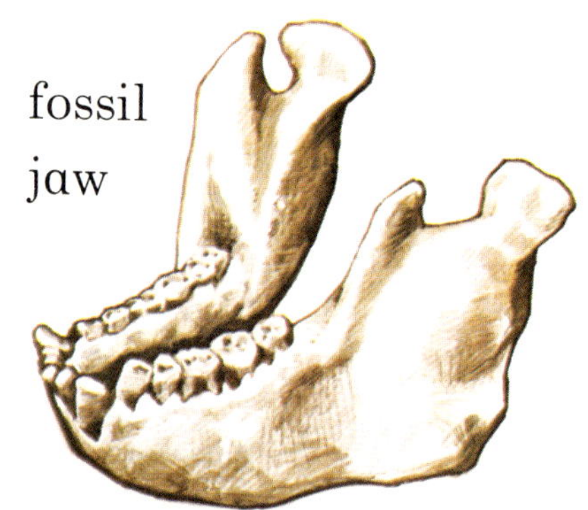
fossil jaw

gigantopithecus

Prehistoric man developed from the apes. Some people thought these prehistoric men were more like the yeti. Perhaps they hadn't died out long ago as scientists believed. Maybe some had fled to out-of-the-way places. There was one way to find out if such creatures existed, scientists said. An expedition should be sent to the Himalayas to look for the yeti's tracks. The fur and scalps the yeti had, and the marks they made should be studied and they should take special equipment to capture a yeti.

Sir Edmund Hillary was asked to lead this expedition. He took cameras and air guns that fired bullets filled with sleep-making drugs. For weeks Hillary searched. He never saw a yeti, but he found tracks. Monks from Pangboche Monastery gave him furs, scalps and even a dried hand. They said these came from yetis.

Hillary studied the tracks carefully. Then he said they were made by wolves or snow leopards. He was able to prove this by following the tracks for some distance and then comparing the tracks which were in the shade with those in the sunlight. In sunlight the tracks looked like those of a large two-footed creature. However, in the shade each large print turned into several small footprints. Hillary could see the separate marks of the animal's front and back legs. When the tracks entered the sunlight they melted. They grew larger and merged into each other. Now little marks became one big footprint.

Next Hillary looked at the objects that the monks had given him. He discovered the furs belonged to the Tibetan blue bear. The scalps were from a rare goat-like antelope in Nepal. The hand was a human's. Even the shrill cries that people had heard, and had claimed were made by the yeti, were probably the sounds of a bird called the mountain chough.

In America, too, people began to study reports of sasquatch more carefully. The showman refused to show his hairy man in ice any more. Perhaps it was because a newspaper said it was made of rubber. The report also said it knew of the man who covered the body with hair. He worked for a wax museum in California.

Scientists studied Patterson's 20-second film carefully. They thought the creature in it moved like a human. They said a man could dress in an ape costume and wait for the camera man. Many bigfoot prints were thought to be fake too. A pair of shoes shaped like giant feet was discovered in a forest hut.

To many people this proved that there was no such thing as a yeti or sasquatch. Yet reliable explorers and many other people had been seeing giant two-legged creatures for years. They saw them long before newspapers became interested in them. These people had nothing to gain by telling lies. Perhaps the few scientists who still believe in the yeti are right when they compare it with the okapi and the coelacanth. The okapi is a small relative of the giraffe. No one believed it existed. Then one day it was discovered in Africa. The coelacanth, a giant fish, was said to have died out millions of years ago. In 1938 one was caught alive in a fisherman's net near Madagascar. Even the gorilla, like the okapi, was thought to be a myth until about 1846. Maybe a large ape-like creature does still exist in the remote parts of the world.